DRAW GALACTIC WORLDS

ROGER LOVELESS

tangerine Press

Project Editor: Treesha R. Vaux
Designer: Treesha R. Vaux
Instructions and Illustrations for Drawing Materials: Nina Kidd

Cover Art: Donato

ISBN 0-439-15397-2

Printed and bound in the United States of America

DB 10 9 8 7 6 5 4 3 2 1

CONTENTS

This book shows you how to draw vehicles, droids, aliens, and cities using a few tools and a lot of imagination.

Each illustration includes step-by-step instructions to help you as you draw. Keep in mind that the final step features only one way the drawing can be finished. Use your imagination to finish each drawing as you wish.

Use a large sheet of paper and make your drawing fill up the space. That way, it's easy to see what you are doing, and it will give you plenty of room to add details.

Experiment with different kinds of lines: Do a light line, then gradually bear down for a wider, darker one. You'll find that just by changing the thickness of a line, your whole picture will look different! Also, try groups of lines, drawing all the lines straight, crisscrossed, curved, or jagged.

Remember that every artist has his or her own style. That's why the pictures you draw won't look exactly like the ones in the book. Instead, they'll reflect your own creative touch.

Most of all, have fun!

WHAT YOU'LL NEED

PAPER

Many kinds of paper can be used for drawing, but some are better than others. Use a large pad of bond paper (or a similar type) for the simpler, more rounded drawings and graph paper for the more technical ones with lots of straight edges. You can find bond and graph paper at an art store. If you are using ink, a dull-finished, coated paper works well.

PENCILS, CHARCOAL, AND PENS

A regular school pencil is fine for the drawings in this book, but try to use one with a soft lead. Pencils with a soft lead are labeled #2; #3 pencils have a hard lead. If you want a thicker lead, ask an art store clerk or your art teacher for an artist's drafting pencil.

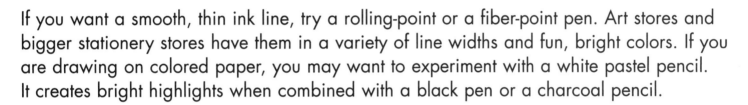

Charcoal works well when you want a very black line, so if you're just starting to draw with charcoal, use a charcoal pencil of medium to hard grade. Use it to rub in shadows, then erase certain areas to make highlights. Work with large pieces of paper, as charcoal is difficult to control in small drawings. And remember that charcoal smudges easily!

If you want a smooth, thin ink line, try a rolling-point or a fiber-point pen. Art stores and bigger stationery stores have them in a variety of line widths and fun, bright colors. If you are drawing on colored paper, you may want to experiment with a white pastel pencil. It creates bright highlights when combined with a black pen or a charcoal pencil.

ERASERS

An eraser is one of your most important tools! Besides removing unwanted lines and cleaning up smudges, erasers can be used to make highlights and textures. Get a soft plastic type (the white ones are good), or for very small areas, a gray kneaded eraser can be helpful. Try not to take off ink with an eraser because it will ruin the drawing paper. If you must take an ink line out of your picture, use liquid whiteout.

OTHER HANDY TOOLS

Facial tissues are helpful for creating soft shadows—just go over your pencil marks with a tissue, gently rubbing the area you want smoothed out. You can also use a Q-Tip® to blend some shaded areas.

You will also need a pencil sharpener, but if you don't have one, rub a small piece of sandpaper against the side of your pencil to keep the point sharp.

A ruler can be very helpful in getting the sharp, straight lines shown in some of these drawings.

You may want to use a compass, if you have one, to help you draw circles for some of the items, but it is not necessary.

Earth and Water City is visited by everyone in the galaxy. It is a center of trade as well as a popular resort. The cascading waterfalls attract life-forms from every corner of the universe.

1. Start by sketching the contour, or outline, of the city. Remember that every drawing begins with shapes. Draw this outline lightly so you can erase it if you need to.

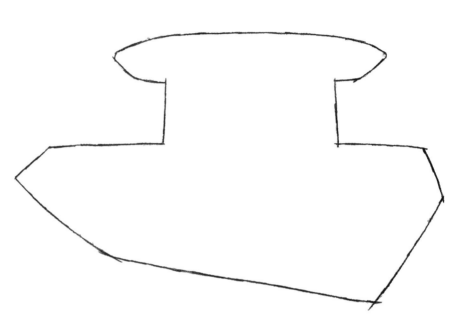

2. Now it is time to build your city. Fill in the shapes of both waterfalls. Find the top of the waterfall in front and draw the central city structure. Fill in the mountains in the distance and the shoreline in the foreground.

3. Draw the support columns at the base of the city structure. Sketch a second line at the top of the city. This will be the outer rim of the central structure. Draw vertical lines at various heights to mark some of the buildings. Begin to create the forests with soft, cloudlike shapes.

4. Finish the support columns, and begin to sketch the buildings. Add some texture to the forests, and detail the shoreline.

5. Add more detail to the buildings. Sketch windows, ventilation panels, and lighting systems on your skyline city. Draw some craft in the water and air.

6. Further detail the forests and waterfalls. Add panel strips to the power tunnel connected at the base. Put details on both the air and water craft. Draw the lines of the ventilation panels on the base of the city.

7. Add detail by shading some areas. Give your buildings windows. Lightly draw reflections in the water.

8. Add as much detail as you want to bring your Earth and Water City to life.

HOVERCRAFT

This hovercraft is very fast and can go straight up and straight across. It hovers about 2 feet above ground and is popular on every planet in the galaxy.

1. Sketch the outline of the hovercraft. Add a horizon line, and indicate some mountains in the background.

2. Fill in the major shapes of the vehicle. Look at the finished illustration to double check your drawing.

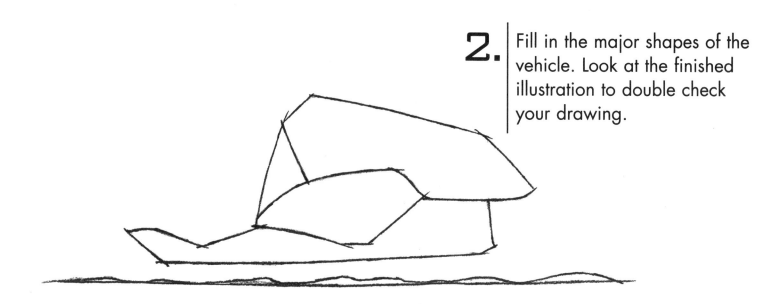

3. Begin to indicate the rounded engine thruster cones at the rear. Draw the front of the air intakes, which are on both sides of the craft. Start to fill in the pilot area.

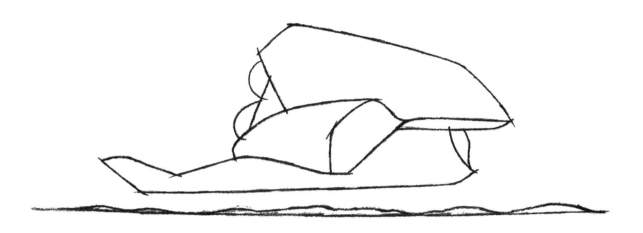

4. Indicate the top, front, and side windows of the pilot housing and the armored belly panel below. Add more detail to the air intakes and the bottom of the craft.

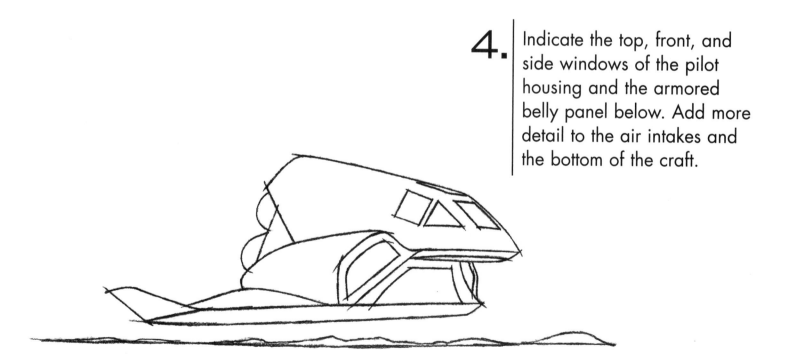

5. Using a ruler, draw some panel lines on the pilot housing. Add detailed lines to the engine thruster cones and air intakes. To create a three-dimensional look, sketch a line going from front to back of the pilot housing in between the windows. Put in antennae, and indicate the circular hover jets on the bottom of the craft.

6. Draw the main thruster engine exhaust and hover jet exhaust. Begin to add some rocks and clouds to create the surroundings. Continue to detail the hovercraft. Erase unneeded lines in the round hover jets.

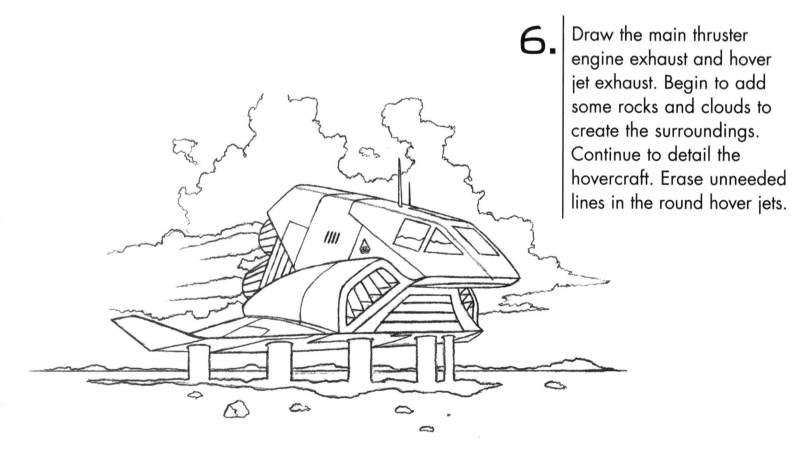

7. Begin to shade your drawing. Start light, adding darker shades gradually. Notice how the exhaust stays white and the shading is on the outside.

8. Finish shading your hovercraft. It is now ready to take off!

The underwater vehicle is a very sleek and super-silent craft. Resembling a skate, or ray, this craft can glide underwater and in space. It is a popular craft in Earth and Water City.

1. Draw the outline of your vehicle. Make the lower wing slightly larger. Sketch a curved horizon line.

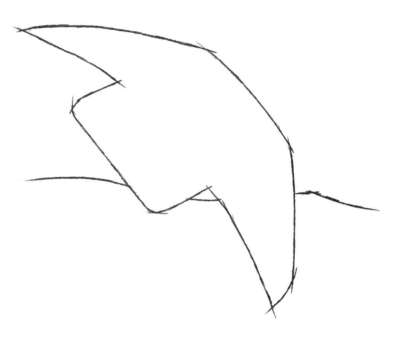

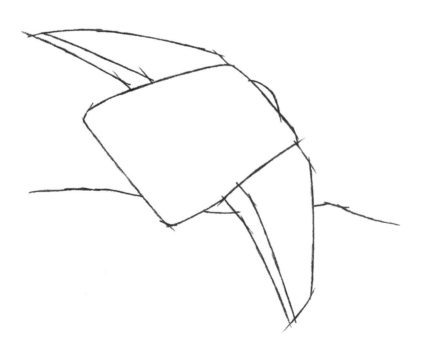

2. Draw the front edges of the wings, and add a rounded shape at the back. This will be the rear engine thruster cone. Create the vehicle's square-shaped body.

3. Curve the front of the body to create the pincer effect. Draw a line above the thruster cone on the main body. This will be the surface radar. Add blast tanks below the wings.

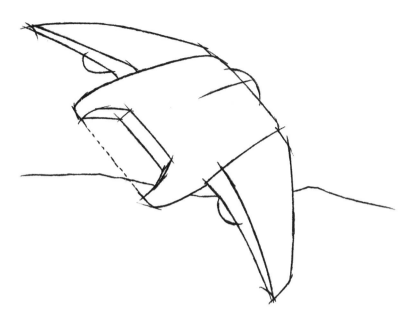

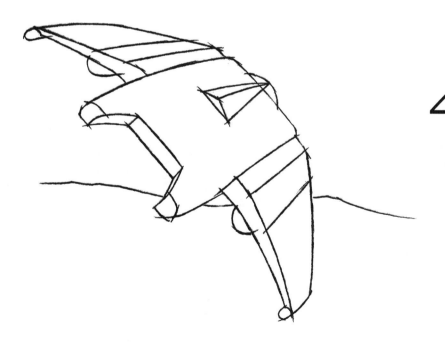

4. Sketch vent panels on both wings. Finish the triangular surface radar. Add small circles to the wing tips. These are the sonar motion detectors. Erase the unneeded guideline on the front of the vehicle.

5. Draw the front wind and water screen on top of the vehicle. Add the pincer vent intake in front. Lightly draw the fish and undersea foliage.

6. Further detail the fish and foliage. Draw panel lines on the wings. Add intake vents on top of each wing. Sketch some detail on the rear thruster cone, then add the exhaust plume.

7. Lightly pencil in the areas to be shaded, including the ground underneath the vehicle. Add some more detail wherever your craft needs it.

8. Continue shading until you've achieved the desired effect. As shown here, try to create the reflective look on the wind and water screen.

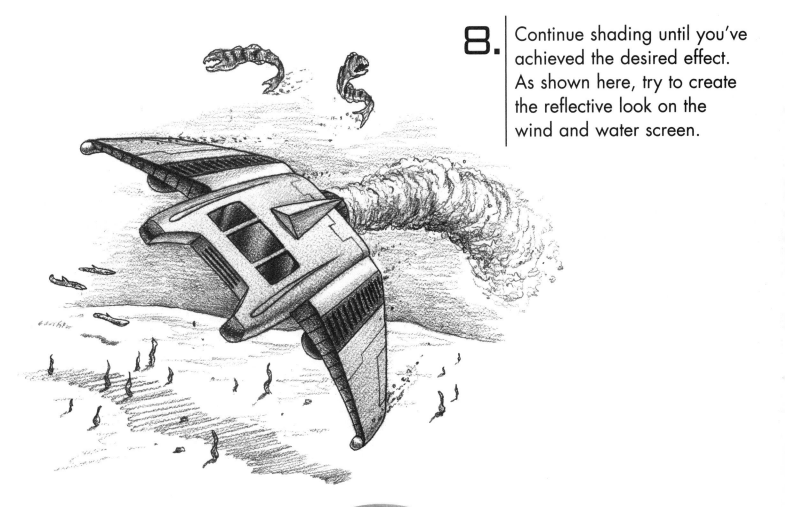

This vehicle is a rough-and-tough, all-terrain monster. It is extremely versatile because of its accordion shape and powerful treads. It is used for transporting cargo and seats six passengers.

1. Sketch the outline of the vehicle. Add a horizon line on either side.

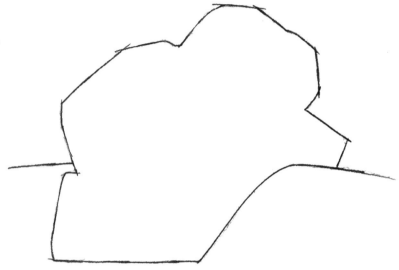

2. Divide the vehicle into its major parts, then fill in those shapes. Think of each piece as part of a puzzle.

3. Fill in the driver's area up front, as well as the column shape below. Add some detail to the upper and lower cargo areas in back. Sketch the rear wheel, or track.

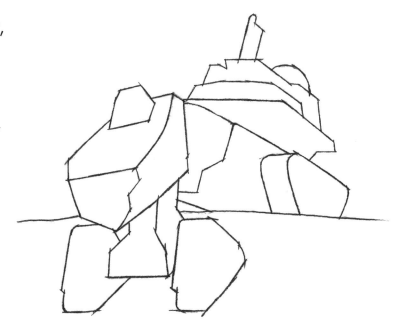

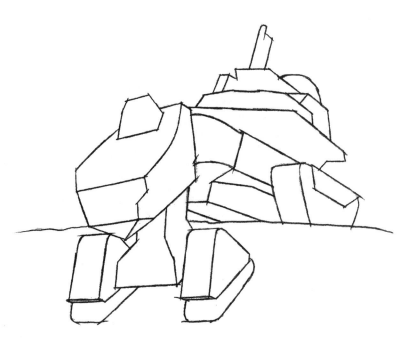

4. Draw the two front and one rear track covers. Sketch the midsection, and continue detailing the cargo area. Draw a line across the driver's area in front.

5. Use your ruler to add lines to the vehicle. Detail the driver's structure in the front. Draw lines to create the accordion effect in the midsection. Add wheels to the tracks and more detail to the upper cargo area.

6. Draw treads on the front and rear tracks. Add the cylinder shapes for axles on the rear tracks. Sketch small panels on the driver and cargo areas. Draw some plant life and track prints on the sand.

7. Lightly add some shading to the vehicle. Remember to leave some areas white in order to create the effect of reflected light.

8. Finish shading your desert transport vehicle. You are now ready to explore any desert terrain!

With the increase of colonization in the galaxy, the demand for food and workers has increased. Droids are very important on each planet and make up a majority of the workforce. This computer-run droid is no exception.

1. Draw the outline of your harvester droid. Try to draw the outline lightly so you can erase it later.

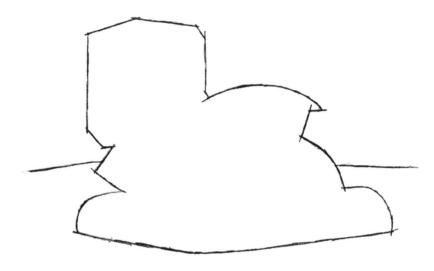

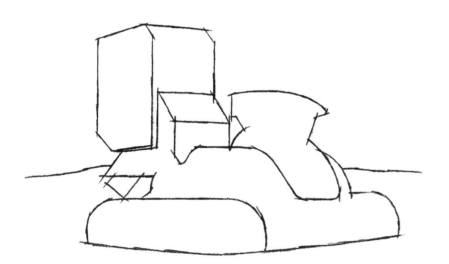

2. Fill in the major sections, such as the baler box at the rear, the treads, the main body, and the control center at the front.

3. Next, fill in the curved body of the droid. Sketch some details on the rear baler box. Add the top of the control center at the front.

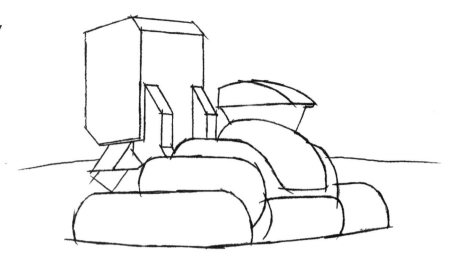

4. Draw the side domes on the baler box and the intake chute. Next, draw the solar positioning dome on the top of the control center. Sketch the tread wheels, along with the two side axles that connect the treads to the main body. Add the front grain intake blades. Erase the bottom edges of your droid and any other unnecessary lines.

5. Sketch the interior of the baler box. Add some grain going up the chute and into the baler box. Sketch some partial bales of grain in the background. Next, draw the tread paddles. Add the ringed planet in the background.

6. Add panel lines to the droid as shown. Finish the tread area and the wheels. Erase extra lines around the treads. Refine the bales of grain, and add some wheat on the ground.

7. Begin to shade your drawing. Use short, vertical strokes to shade the droid. Use looser lines to shade the wheat on the ground.

8. Finish shading your droid. Try diagonal lines when shading the axle to give your droid a metallic look.

Each planet has millions of these construction droids. They can work around the clock, require no food or rest, and get the job done fast.

1. Sketch the droid outline, along with the wooden beams. You may want to use a ruler for the beams.

2. Divide the droid at its waist. Add the wrench arm and drill arm. Draw the smaller droid piece floating above. Sketch some beams on the ground.

3. Begin to shape the tracks and base of the feet. Add hatchway doors on top of the main body, and give the body dimension. Draw sides on the smaller droid, and add its tether line. Put a beam in the wrench hand, and shape the drill hand. Erase unnecessary lines.

4. Add lines on the track and lower body to give your droid a three-dimensional look. Draw the body cavity on top of your droid. This is the smaller droid housing. Sketch details on the smaller droid. Add a second tether line to the drill hand. Give the drill hand some detail.

5. Draw sides on the beams. Add more detail to the smaller droid. Using the guidelines, sketch three tether lines to the wrench hand. Draw vents on the top hatches. Add panel details to the body and the sides of the tracks.

6. Next, sketch cables at the back of the main body, and add detail inside the body cavity. Add vertical lines to the waist, and draw treads on the tracks. Sketch segmented lines on the cables of the arms, and detail the middle of the wrench hand. Add sparks coming from the drill hand, and place a crosspiece in the upper-left corner of the two left beams.

7. Begin to shade your drawing. Start with light shading, then move on to use darker shading in certain areas.

8. Continue shading as you wish. Don't forget to create light shadows on the floor. Your construction droid is now ready to go to work!

This space station is unique in its design. It is equipped with powerful engine thrusters that enable it to orbit through space and also land on planets.

1. Sketch the outline of the dual space station and add a horizon line.

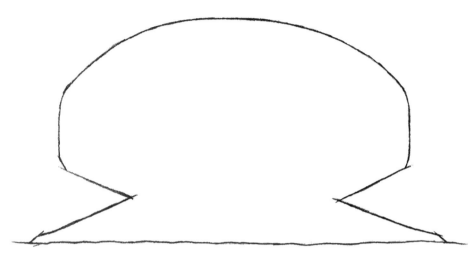

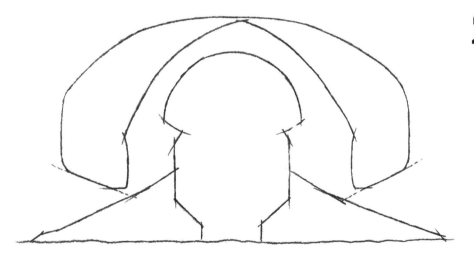

2. Use a ruler to find the center of the station. Sketch the mushroom shape of the main structure. Add the outline of the curved cross-beams on top.

3. Next, fill in the cross-beams on top of the structure. Draw the four engines extending from the beams. Use a ruler to draw an X connecting the four engines. Sketch two of the legs as shown. Begin to erase guidelines.

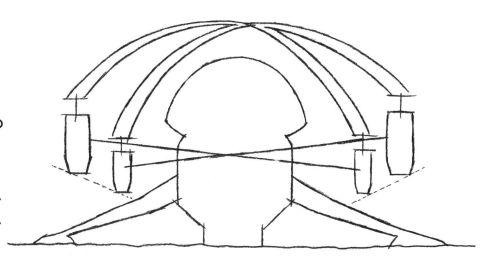

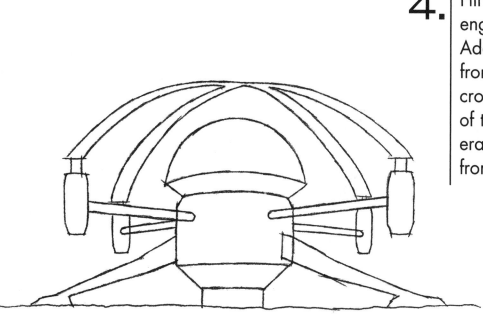

4. Fill in the X to make the engine maintenance tunnels. Add another connecting line from each engine to the cross-beams. Sketch the base of the space station, and erase the two dotted lines from Step 3.

5. Add sides to the cross-beam arches. Draw dividing lines on the main body to show the many sections. Add the other two legs. Give the legs a three-dimensional look and dividing lines. Begin to indicate the surrounding landscape. Start to detail the engines, and erase extra lines.

6. Draw windows on the main body, legs, and tunnels. Add vents to the body and engines. Sketch a semicircle line in the dome. Add some detail to the rocky landscape.

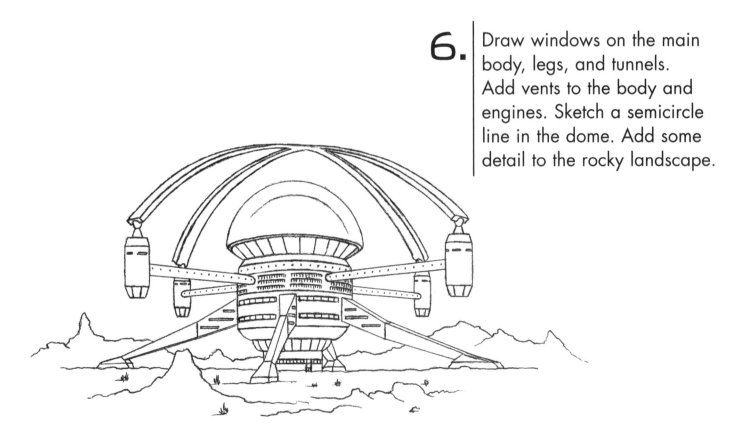

7. Create highlights on the dome. Begin to add shading to the whole space station and the landscape.

8. Finish shading the necessary areas. Remember to leave some areas white for effect.

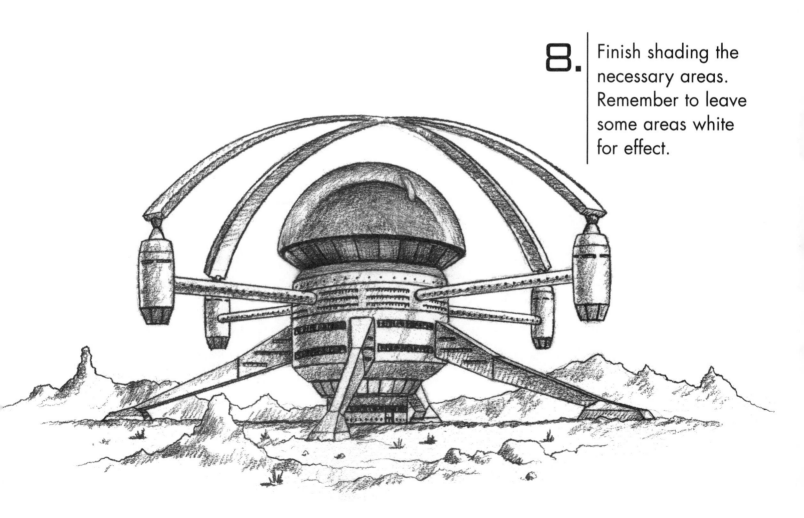

Not only is he ugly, but this alien is also extremely ruthless. His large shape is quite deceiving, for when challenged, this alien can move! What's more, his razor-sharp stinger is coated with deadly venom.

1. Sketch the outline of the alien emperor. Pay close attention to the size of the various shapes.

2. Begin to sketch the tail, the legs, and the head. Look at the final step to identify the many parts. Draw the lines light enough so you can alter them later.

3. Draw both of the arms, then add the scepter. Next, sketch your alien's fingers and toes. Erase unneeded lines as you go.

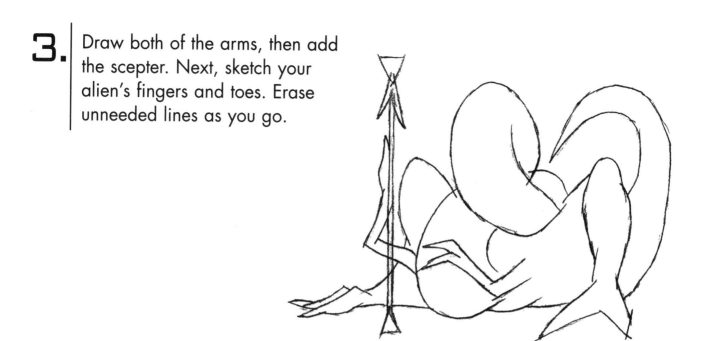

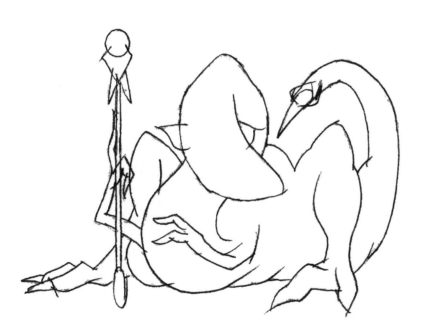

4. Refine the toes and the fingers. Detail the end of the tail, or the base of the stinger. Add detail to the scepter. Sketch the alien emperor's eye sockets.

5. Continue to refine the shape of the hands, and add long toenails to the feet. Detail the stinger at the end of the tail, as well as the scepter. Sketch the head structure, and add nostrils. Add eyes in the eye sockets.

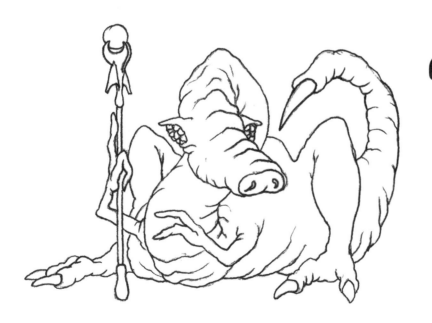

6. Next, add textured lines all over the skin's surface. Finish drawing the fingers and toes. Add circles in his eyes to create a multi-eyeball look.

7. Draw tigerlike stripes on the skin. Add dots and other details to create the skin's bumpy look. Begin to shade your alien as shown.

8. Continue shading until the desired effect is obtained. Your alien emperor is ready to rule!

Although she is not the most attractive queen in the universe, the spider queen is much loved. She is a fair and kind-hearted ruler and has maintained peace and prosperity throughout her kingdom.

1. Draw the outline of the queen and her throne. Use a compass, if you have one, to draw the throne.

2. Fill in the rest of the shapes. Check your placement against this and the final drawing.

3. Next, draw the queen's robe. Outline the arms, hands, and feet.

4. Sketch the spider legs and the queen's hooked teeth. (Only five of the eight legs are visible.) Give your queen some fingers and toes. Erase extra lines as you draw.

5. Fill in the robe by adding some folds as shown. Sketch the eyes and mouth, and add the baby spider in the queen's left hand. Start to refine the throne and its base. Detail the queen's boots.

6. Now detail the queen's head and face. Add a striped pattern to her stockings and the ridge of her head. Draw webbing on her throne and some lines on its base.

7. Start to shade the spider queen. Use your imagination when adding detail. Your spider queen does not need to look exactly like this one.

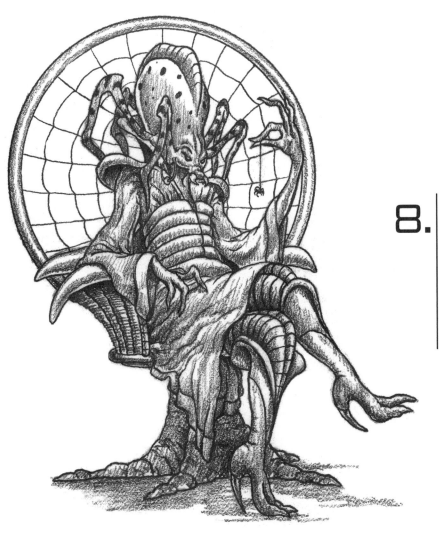

8. Add some final shading and any other finishing touches you wish. Remember to leave some areas light for highlights. The spider queen is ready to greet her people.

This combat alien is a very powerful fighter. All four of his arms are equally strong and lethal weapons on their own. Combat aliens win almost every battle and are very sore losers.

1. Look at the shapes of the finished drawing, and then draw the outline as shown here.

2. Add some form to the legs and feet. Think of the torso, arms, and head as basic shapes, then create them.

3. Now turn the shapes into your combat alien. Render the head and neck. Next, sketch the arms and hands. Erase any extra lines.

4. Further shape the head and jaw areas, and begin to form the mouth. Give him some ears and more fingers. The combat alien is very strong, so sketch some muscles in his arms and shoulders. Draw his belt, and begin to detail his legs. Sketch a gun holster on his thigh, and start to detail his backpack.

5. Add his eyes, nose, and lips. Detail his holster and belt. Fill in pockets on his pants, and give his boots some detail. Refine the outline of your alien.

6. Complete his facial features by adding some teeth and wrinkles. Draw buckles on his boots and a camouflage pattern on his pants. Detail his backpack and the strap across his chest.

7. Begin to add light shading all over your alien.

8. Complete your combat alien by darkening some areas more than others. Give him a shadow on the ground. Your combat alien is ready for action!

A space station of this size is quite a sight. It is a self-contained unit that has a school, a greenhouse the size of a football field, and an Olympic-size training pool. If you are orbiting space, this is the ship to be on.

1. Using your graph paper, list numbers 1 through 21 from left to right, and letters A through U from top to bottom. This grid will help you to map out your drawing and can be erased later. Sketch the outline of the space station. Use the grid to find the location of particular parts. For example, the front point of the ship is in the middle of H-21, while the point of the back wing is in F-3.

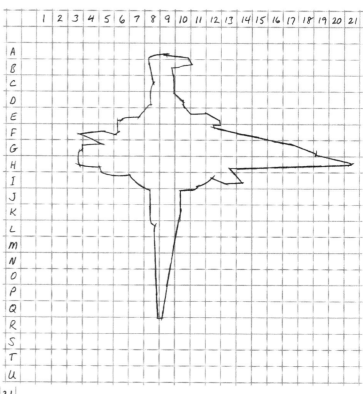

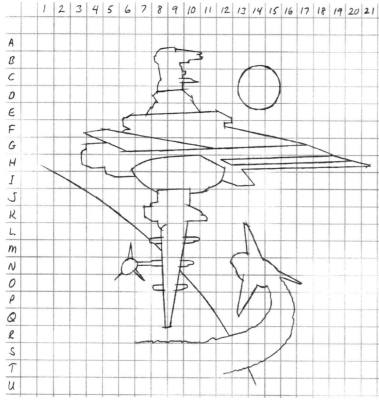

2. Using the same method, sketch in the outlines of the small shuttlecraft and its exhaust. Begin to add detail to the space station. Sketch in the curved line that is the planet's surface, then add a moon. Also add the tiny spacecraft at the left.

3. Complete the main body of the space station. Define the shuttle wings. Add other details throughout the drawing to give it a three-dimensional look.

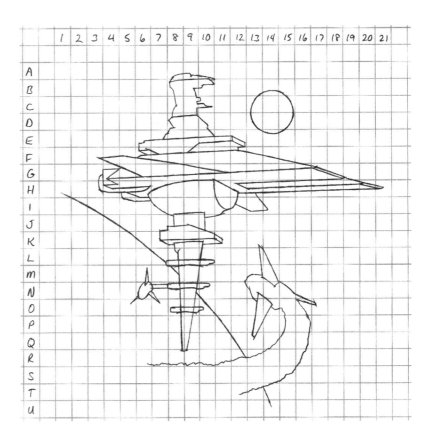

4. Next, sketch the back of the shuttle to define its shape, and add a window in front. Detail the tower on top of the space station. Draw some panels on the entire station. Give the moon a crescent shape, and detail the tiny shuttle.

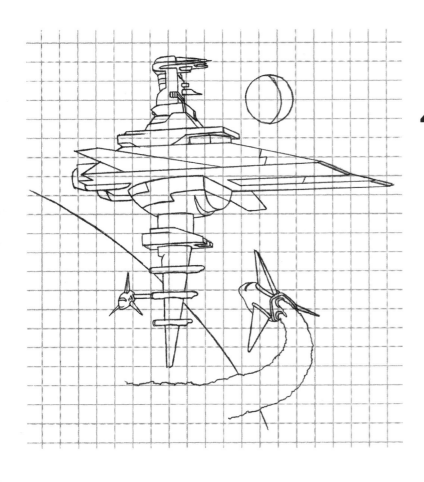

5. Add some windows to the shuttles, and refine the exhaust. Draw the rest of the panel lines on the ship, and further detail the tower. Add small windows on the main body. Sketch some clouds on the planet surface, and add a shadow on the moon.

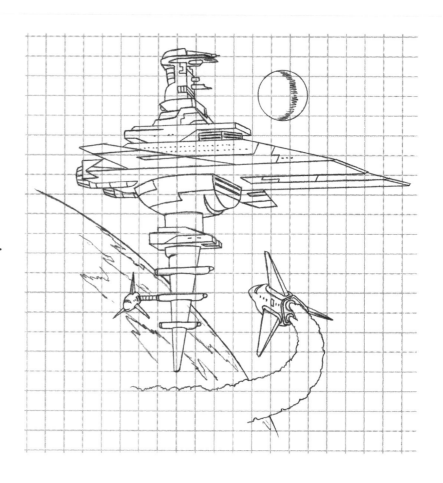

6. Complete your drawing by shading as shown. Notice how the shading is darker under the main body of the space station. This is because the moon's reflected light creates shadows.

METEOR BLASTER

Meteor showers are common occurrences, and every planet has a few of these blaster droids. Its armor is tougher than steel, and its radar can detect a meteor before it has entered the atmosphere.

1. On your graph paper, write numbers 1 through 23 from left to right, and letters A through Q from top to bottom. Draw the outline of the droid using this grid. Draw lightly when you are sketching the outline location.

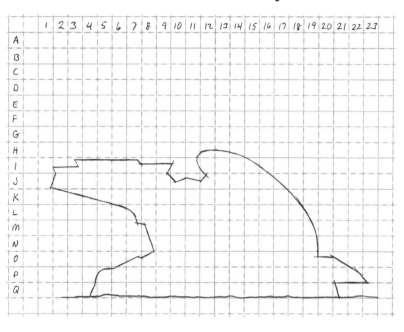

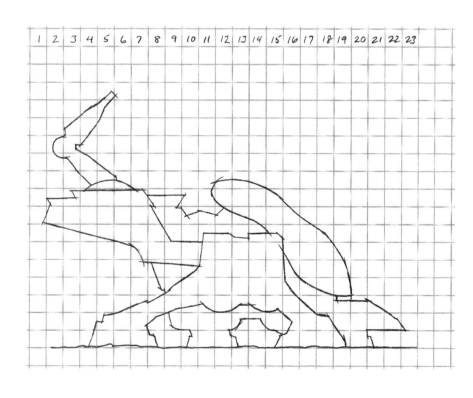

2. Sketch in the outline of the other shapes. Add the blaster cannon, located between C-5 and H-5.

3. Next, sketch the bottoms of the feet and the bottom of the main body. Continue to create the different parts inside the meteor blaster's outline.

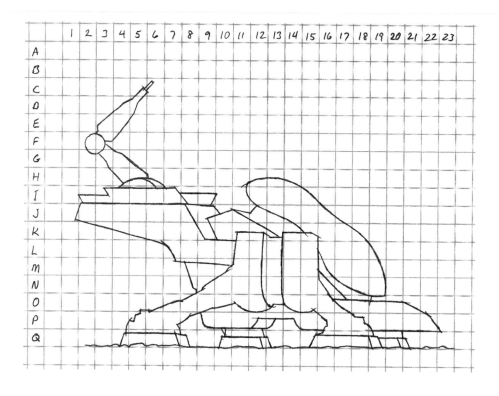

4. Detail the feet and legs. Add the oval shape on the rear of the main body. This is the armored radar. Finish the main body area, and give the cannon more detail.

5. Complete the details on the legs and feet, and add panel lines all over your droid. Finish the blaster cannon, then add antennae. Draw some incoming meteors!

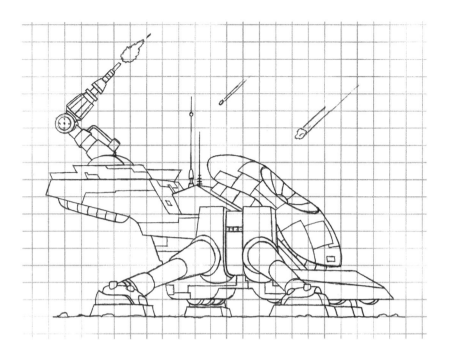

6. Complete your meteor blaster by adding shading and highlights where you want. Perhaps draw a meteor being blasted by the cannon.

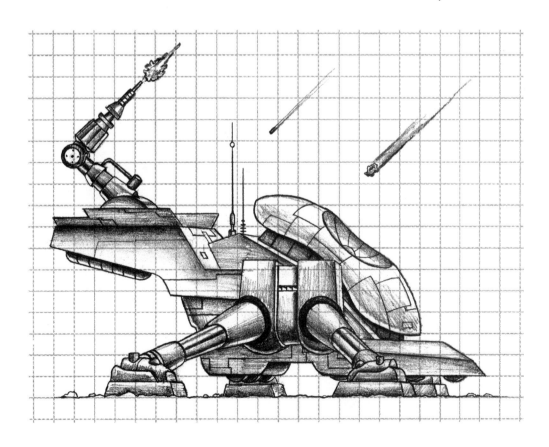

This huge power and energy control center is responsible for the workings of every droid and mainframe computer in Earth and Water City.

1. Using your graph paper, write the numbers 1 through 23 from left to right, and letters A through K from top to bottom. Sketch the outline of your control center.

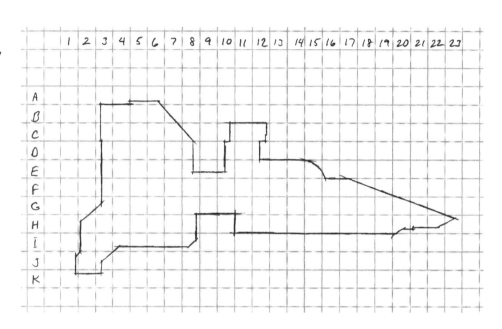

2. Begin to add outlines of the major shapes. Draw the gravity maker, which is located between I-11 and I-15. Add the surface monitor, located between K-2 and K-5.

3. Draw various panel lines throughout your ship. Sketch as many details on your craft as you would like.

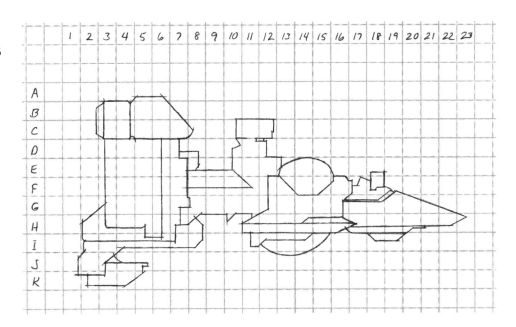

4. Add more panel lines and other details. Draw the front windows on the lower deck of the ship's nose, located between G-19 and G-22 on the grid.

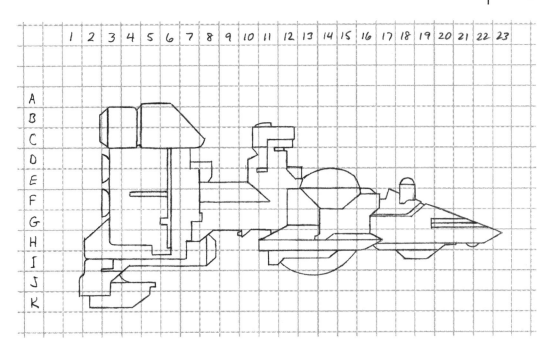

5. Draw some more windows at the bottom left, and keep adding panel lines. The more detail you can add, the better your control center will look.

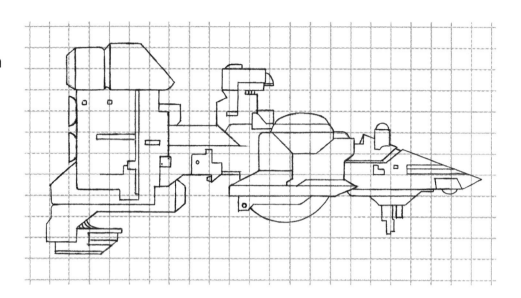

6. Next, add filter lines on the bottom of the gravity maker. Complete all panel lines and other details on your ship.

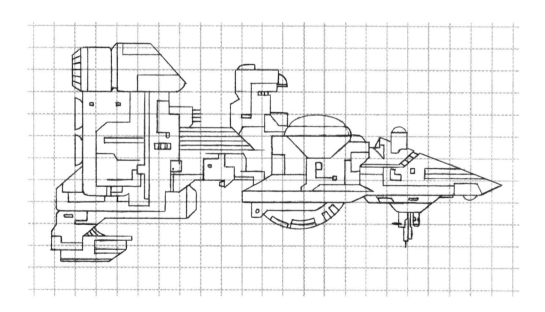

7. Start to shade your control center. Try using short, diagonal lines in some areas while leaving other areas white.

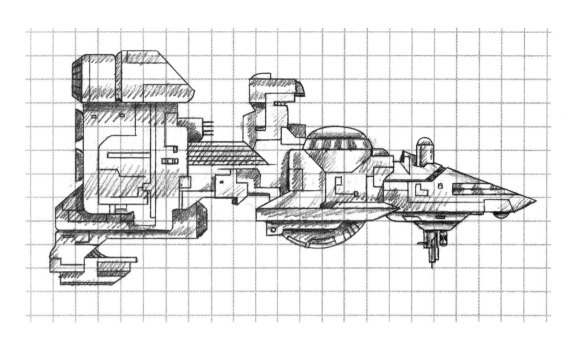

8. Use a darker pencil stroke to complete the shading of your control center. To blend some areas, try using a Q-Tip® until you get the desired effect.

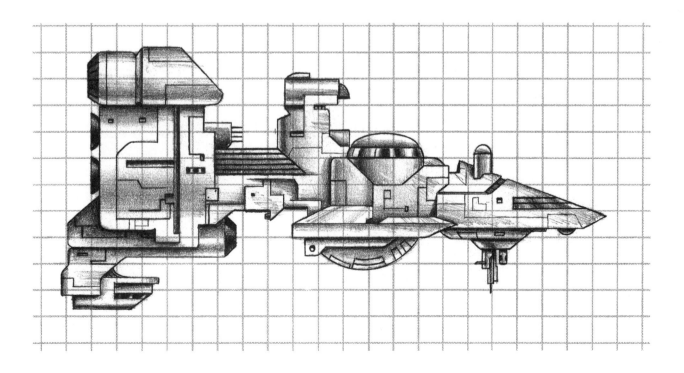

Before a new planet is colonized, mission collector droids are sent ahead to gather samples of the soil or rock formations to ensure that the planet is inhabitable.

1. Using your graph paper, write numbers 1 through 12 from left to right, and letters A through S from top to bottom. Sketch the outline of the droid. Create the outlines of the arms and pincers.

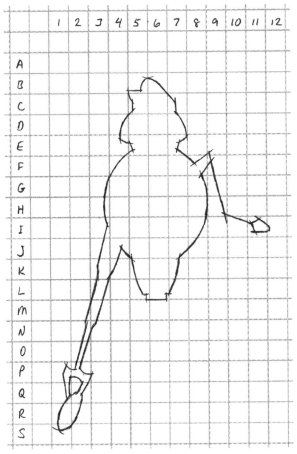

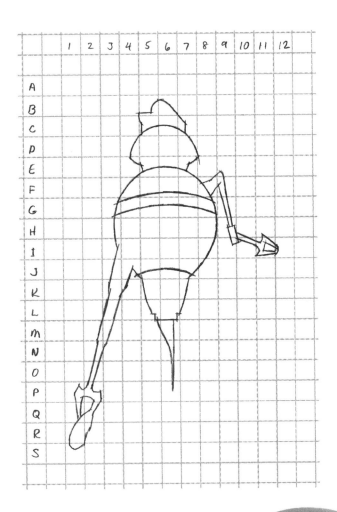

2. If you have a compass, use it to construct the head and body. Sketch the curved lines of the mid- and bottom sections. Outline the stinger probe, which is located between M-6 and P-6 on the grid. Detail the pincer and arm on the right.

3. Add the radar device, infrared light, and one antenna on top of the head. Sketch details on the arms and pincers. Further form the hatch opening on the belly compartment. Draw the two other small stinger probes.

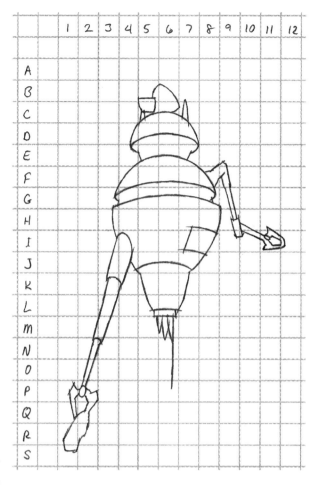

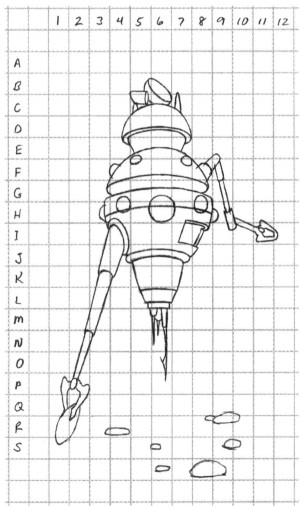

4. Fill in a second line around the head dome for thickness. Add another line on the belly hatch as well. Detail the three probes on the bottom of the droid. Draw the five round lenses of the optical sensors. Detail other items as shown here, and draw some rocks on the ground below.

5. Finish the structural details on top, including the antennae. Add four suspension rods between the upper and lower halves of the main body. Draw three identification lights above the probes on the bottom of the droid.

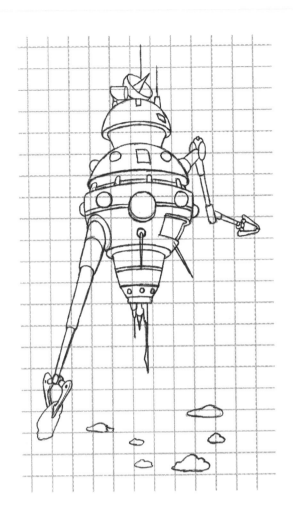

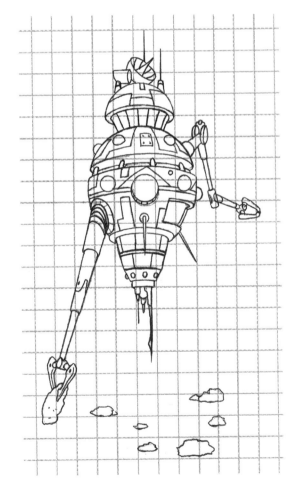

6. Sketch panel lines on the head, neck, main body, and lower section of the droid. Add as much detail as you would like.

7. Begin to shade your droid. Remember to highlight the optical lenses and the tops of the head and belly domes. Add the droid's shadow on the ground.

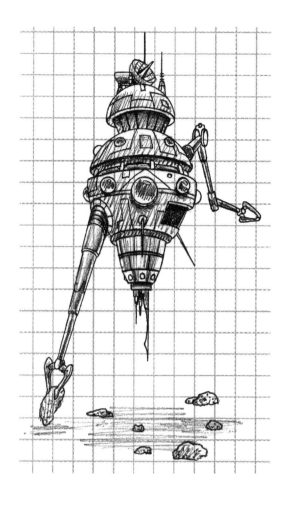

8. Finish shading your droid to give it a three-dimensional look. Notice how the belly hatch is black.

Desert City is a spectacular accomplishment. The environmental domes are over 2 feet thick and able to withstand the fiercest sand storm. Large tunnels connect the three domes.

1. Using your graph paper, write numbers 1 through 26 from left to right, and letters A through N from top to bottom. Lightly sketch the outline of the city as shown.

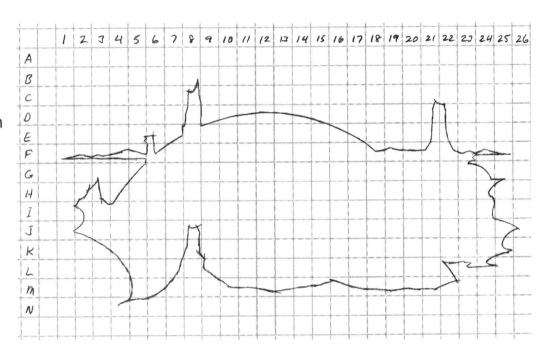

2. Next, draw the outlines of the three environmental domes and the desert landscape. Use the letters and numbers of the graph paper to place your domes correctly.

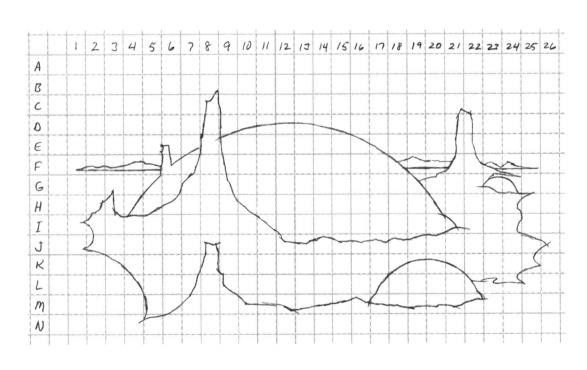

3. Add connecting tunnels between the domes. Draw the rim on the base of each dome. Begin to draw foliage and buildings inside the domes.

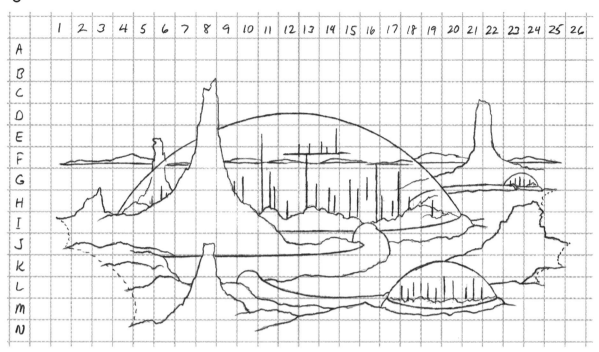

4. Add clouds and a sun. Start to add some detail to the surrounding terrain. Draw the outlines of the buildings. Erase unneeded lines as you go.

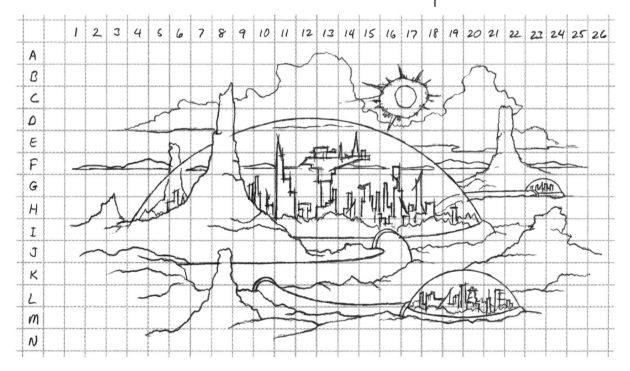

5. Next, detail the buildings. Add roads with support beams inside the tunnels. Refine the sun and clouds. Begin to create the airport at the upper right.

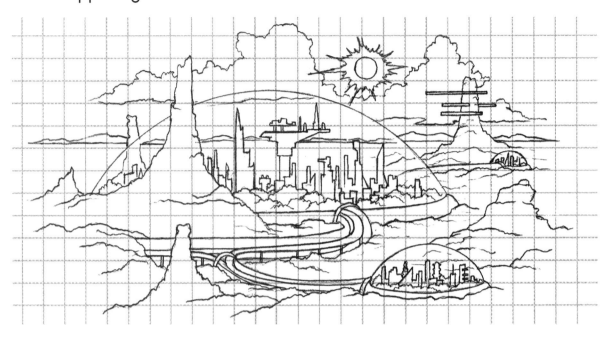

6. Finish detailing the landscape and the foliage. Put windows on the buildings. Further detail the tunnels, and add vehicles on the roads. Add support beams and airplanes to the airport.

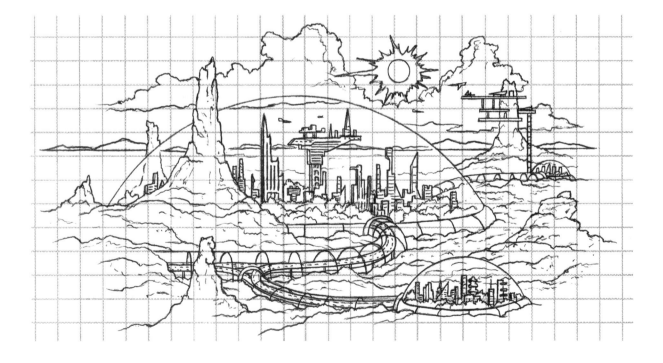

7. Begin to shade your drawing. Sketch shadows on the land, sky, and left side of all the buildings.

8. Try to keep your final image clean and crisp. Put as much detail and shading as you want in your drawing. You're now the mayor of your own desert city!

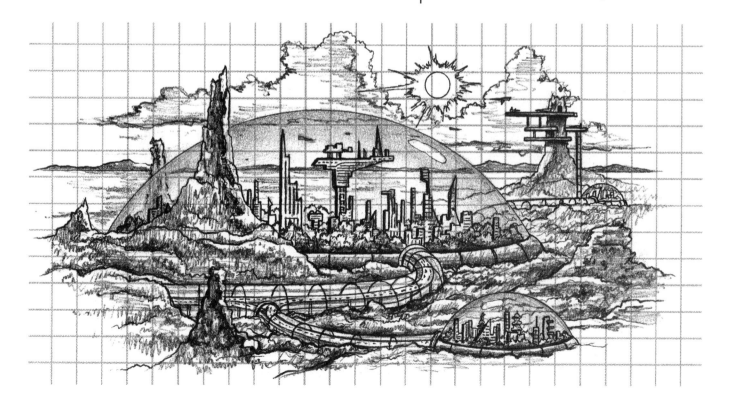

Once you have completed a drawing, you may want to put your creature, city, or vehicle in a setting. For many of your illustrations, the background can be outer space, but you can add all sorts of things to make the scenery interesting. Use your imagination! Here are some suggestions for creating different settings.

MAGAZINE BACKGROUNDS

If you like to cut and paste, ask your family for some old magazines you can use. Cut out pictures of different patterns and trim them so they're shaped like craters, rocks, a cave, or even an alien cityscape. This will give your picture an interesting abstract look. And you don't have to fill the entire page. A few groupings to the side or below your main drawing will give the impression of a whole scene.

PAINTED BACKGROUNDS

You don't need a paintbrush to add painted backgrounds! To create small craters on a planet's surface, dip the end of a drinking straw into some paint and print tiny indentation pockets around your image. You can make smaller craters by using the ends of tiny pieces of macaroni, or bigger ones with large pieces. Cut a piece of sponge, dip it in paint, and stamp it onto your picture to create a rock texture. A crumpled piece of waxed paper or a paper towel can achieve the same effect. Be sure not to get these too wet, though, or they won't work well. Look around the house for other printing tools, such as old wooden spools, corrugated cardboard, or cut pieces of Styrofoam®.

TEXTURED BACKGROUNDS

If you want to create a textured background, you'll need to draw your space alien, city, or vehicle on a thin piece of paper. Place a textured object (such as sandpaper) under the section of your paper where you want the texture to appear. Now get a pencil with a soft lead. Using the side of the pencil lead, rub lightly and evenly over the area.

SHADOWED BACKGROUNDS

By adding shadows in the right places, your illustrations will leap off the page! Imagine where the shadow of your alien, city, or vehicle would fall underneath itself. Then fill in those areas with a dark pencil. You might want to add shadows to some of the rocks or background scenery, too. When adding shadows to your backgrounds, remember that sunlight is different at different times of the day. Morning and late-afternoon light make objects cast very long shadows. Whenever the sun is directly overhead, the shadows cast are very short.